Alpha Male for Beginners

Act Boldly and Become the Man You Were Meant to Be

The Complete Beginners Guide to Becoming an Alpha Male

Disclaimer
- Although the author and publisher have made every effort to ensure that the information in this book was correct at press time, the author and publisher do not assume and hereby disclaim any liability to any party for any loss, damage, or disruption caused by errors or omissions, whether such errors or omissions result from negligence, accident, or any other cause.
- This book is not intended as a substitute for the medical advice of physicians. The reader should regularly consult a physician in matters relating to his/her health and particularly with respect to any symptoms that may require diagnosis or medical attention.

Copyright 2014 by LOVE AND LIVE LIFE TO THE EXTREME FULLEST PUBLISHING- All rights reserved.

This document is geared towards providing exact and reliable information in regards to the topic and issue covered. The publication is sold with the idea that the publisher is not required to render accounting, officially permitted, or otherwise, qualified services. If advice is necessary, legal or professional, a practiced individual in the profession should be ordered.

- From a Declaration of Principles which was accepted and approved equally by a Committee of the American Bar Association and a Committee of Publishers and Associations.

In no way is it legal to reproduce, duplicate, or transmit any part of this document in either electronic means or in printed format. Recording of this publication is strictly prohibited and any storage of this document is not allowed unless with written permission from the publisher. All rights reserved.

The information provided herein is stated to be truthful and consistent, in that any liability, in terms of inattention or otherwise, by any usage or abuse of any policies, processes, or directions contained within is the solitary and utter responsibility of the recipient reader. Under no circumstances will any legal responsibility or blame be held against the publisher for any reparation, damages, or monetary loss due to the information herein, either directly or indirectly.

Respective authors own all copyrights not held by the publisher.

The information herein is offered for informational purposes solely, and is universal as so. The presentation of the information is without contract or any type of guarantee assurance.

The trademarks that are used are without any consent, and the publication of the trademark is without permission or backing by the trademark owner. All trademarks and brands within this book are for clarifying purposes only and are the owned by the owners themselves, not affiliated with this document.

Have Any Issues With This Book? Contact Randy at Randycfo@triggerhealthyhabits.com For Any Concerns About Quality, Copyright, Trademark, Or any issues or concerns you may have.

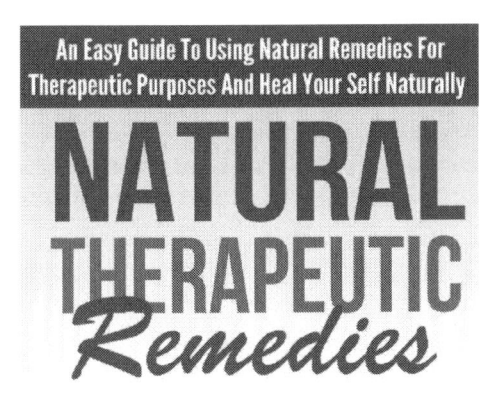

Your FREE Gift
Click Here

As a way of saying thank you,

Get your free natural therapeutic remedies report by clicking below.

What you'll receive

Enjoy the rest of the book!

Click here to get your Natural Therapeutic Remedies Report

The Benefits Of Short Reads,

Our Main Mission Is To Provide You With Quality Content In A Short Period Of Time, We Strive To Make Our Books Short And To The Point. These Days Who Has The Time To Read A Big Long Book? We Do Not Write Fiction Books, We Want To Help As Many People As Possible By Providing Them These Handbooks To Help Better Their Lives . We Hope You Enjoy This Kindle Short Reads E-Book

Contents

- Chapter 1: Introduction 8
  - Why I Am Writing This Book 8
- Chapter 2: Characteristics of Alpha Males 9
  - Physical Aspects 9
  - Confident .... **Error! Bookmark not defined.**
  - Competitive .... **Error! Bookmark not defined.**
  - Progress .... **Error! Bookmark not defined.**
  - Leadership 9
  - Summary of Alpha Males 9
- Chapter 3: How to become the Alpha Male 10
  - Physical Aspects 10
  - Confidence 10
  - Competitiveness 11
  - Progress .... **Error! Bookmark not defined.**
  - Leadership .... **Error! Bookmark not defined.**
  - Summary of "How To" 11
- Chapter 4: Benefits of Being the Alpha Male 12
  - Individually 12
  - Socially .... **Error! Bookmark not defined.**
  - Professionally 12
  - Summary of Benefits 13
- Conclusion 14

Chapter 1: Introduction

In a pack of wolves, they are all led by the alpha male. It is this one wolf's decision making that allows the pack to eat, to stay protected, to survive. This is true across the animal kingdom though most observations acknowledge the canine alpha male. Human beings, as animals are not an exception to this. Mankind has excelled over other beasts because of our ability to excel at these animalistic traits and the alpha male gene is certainly among that.

Everyone has seen *the* movie where a group of "tough guys" huddle around just one person as their unspoken leader. FIghtclub members venerate Tyler Durden, played by Brad Pitt. The movie 300 was lofted at the box office because of uplifting speeches by Leonidas (Gerard Butler) that had every man in the crowd's blood boiling for a fight. Lord of the Ring characters storm into epic battles behind Aragorn. Dating back to when John Travolta starred in Grease and his crew was at his left and right. And even further back.

This is one area of Hollywood dramatization that accurately displays (maybe embellishes a little) the leader of the pack. This person always seems to have an air around them, a sense of cool, an innate show of manliness, a motivator of the masses, and a born leader.

Some idolize this characteristic, some think it is a fictional part of storytelling and others have this trait. We've already seen how this trait has flowed from the animal kingdom into human development and history is covered with realistic proof. Foraging tribes to emerging nations were brought together not just on their own but together with someone as their figurehead.

The Greeks flocked behind Alexander. The Romans behind Caesar. Genghis Kahn led the conquering Mongols. The Spanish behind Ferdinand. The French and British behind their kings. Americans behind Washington. More recently though, these alpha males have been paid handsomely by absolutely gigantic global corporations to head them as the company's CEO or by sports teams they lead, women are attracted to them and parties are centered around them

Why I Am Writing This Book

The reason I am writing this is not for a history lesson or to namedrop Hollywood stars. Before I made mention of a few characters from the history books just to show that this has always existed. I am writing this book because the latter half of my statement above; for how those alpha males are being treated now. It may be a stretch to say that you'll soon be able to become the CEO of a Fortune 500 company but it wouldn't be to say that you'll find success closer at hand.

I want you to realize the benefits of being able to not just promote yourself as an alpha male but how to live it. Allowing yourself to capitalize on your inner alpha male will propel you individually, socially and professionally. Breaking, not away from the pack, but above it is what I want each and every one of you to do. I don't want you to live lives of mediocrity, rather I want you to lead the way for others. Reaching your full ability and self-esteem is what the alpha male really leads to. Achieve it.

Chapter 2: Characteristics of Alpha Males

The benefits of being an alpha male are endless. I will describe some to you now but keep in mind the most important benefits that an alpha male has are those traits that you can't quite say. There is no word to really describe it but all feel it in their presence. These characteristics we can't describe here but we can certainly build towards.

Physical Aspects

Let's look first at the most simple, animalistic traits that we can use to describe the alpha character. Alpha males' physique is the first thing that comes across your field of vision. The best way to describe them is sturdy. They are strong enough to know they are capable in all situations (this knowing will be discussed later) but they are not too weighted down by their muscle. There is a balance between strength and weakness because an alpha male is not a bull – someone that is completely headstrong without any strength in their head – and they are not a cow – feminine in instincts and nurturing. Wolf and man alike, they have the testosterone needed to make those around them feel it and that is the starting point for it all.

Leadership

We already mentioned that alpha males are born leaders and that they are. They don't manage and dictate to others but encourage and motivate them. They do not demand respect, rather others feel that they have earned it. In the portrayals in the previous chapter, we looked at how the alpha male is always surrounded by people following him. This is the same with an alpha male wolf because they are followed directly by their pack. Think about what it takes for that devotion. If you are a follower now, why do you follow others? What do they do for you? These questions are important because each person following another must receive something in order to follow them. If there are no gains for these person, there is no point. Is it safety? Is it wisdom? What is it? It really could be anything that someone could gain from the alpha male.

Summary of Alpha Males

It is important to still realize some of the other intangibles related to alpha males. In addition to the abovementioned traits, go back to the celebrities and famous people of history I mentioned earlier and consider what it was about them that really set them apart. Think about people you've come across personally that you consider to be an alpha male.

Study them. Understand some of the more intricate characteristics. Pick what you think is important and learn to apply that.

Chapter 3: How to become the Alpha Male

Once you understand the attributes of an alpha male, it is easy to recognize what you need to do in order to achieve this. Let's look point-by-point to see how you can achieve this.

Physical Aspects

Remember they are firm. You need to support yourself likewise. A toned body is only part of this and the other part is posture, chin placement and expressions. An alpha male stands tall among others and holds his chin level. He doesn't look down at others nor dream away in the sky. A stern face with slight yet solid features is the best way.

So make sure that you get to the gym as often as possible. Your overall health will thank you, your body will look better and your posture will increase. Additionally, strenuous activity naturally bolsters your body's testosterone production. Like canine's can smell the hormones of others, people will be able to pick up on this masculine hormone pulsing through your body.

First impressions usually set the tone for your entire time knowing people. Unfortunately, the first thing that people take in is appearance. Because of this, your physical presence must be perfect and all else stems from this. If you do not look confident, people will not believe you are. If you do not look intelligent, people will not believe you are. And this continues. On and on.

It is extremely important to act and dress the part at hand. Dress like you are intelligent and people will believe you. Position yourself confident and people will believe you are. Show that you are physically capable and literally embody a competitive spirt and people will believe you are. Show you can lead with your physique and people will believe that you can lead in all else. This is just your first show, the actions that come to follow will be how you continue setting this standard.

Confidence

Confidence walks hand and hand with physical attributes at times. Good posture, chin level and facial expressions show that you walk without doubt or pity. Furthermore, you need to remove doubt from your life so that you are more confident in yourself and so that others become more confident in you as well.

There are two ways to express confidence in conversation and that is to speak loudly and knowledgably. When I say loud, I don't want you screaming but more importantly you can't be whispering. Your voice must be firm and unwavering. Think about it, if someone is confident about what they are talking about, do they mind if other people hear it? The answer is no, everyone can hear but stop short of speaking at an obnoxious level.

Additionally, if you have a sense of knowing about the subject at hand, people will take you as an expert, as the alpha in the conversation. Don't stick your two cents in on everything, especially if you don't know about it. Stick to what you know and build that confidence with everyone and build your knowledge into other subjects.

Do not falter in your speech either. This may not be easy at first if you are not a natural speaker but it is possible to get past this. When you are speaking and make a mistake, do not fix it. Continue like there is not a problem. If you go back and fix speech it becomes that much more noticeable. Eventually, you will make fewer and fewer mistakes as you speak.

Competitiveness

Progression is key. You need to always be willing to progress. You also need to invite change into your life. Do not resist change, welcome it and master it. Change is exceptionally important at the beginning, specifically if you are not anywhere close to being considered an alpha male with your social group.

For those that are far from being considered the alpha male of their group of friends this may be the most difficult part of this entire conversion. You need to make a change, although it doesn't have to be permanent. While you are putting all these other steps together, begin to take part in a new social setting. One where the people around you see you as the alpha male from the get-go rather than changing people's minds later. You can always go back to your friends and after a short absence you'll receive the "Wow!" response when you go back. They'll have noticed your changes.

Summary of "How To"

By fully submerging yourself in your pursuit of alpha male, you will have to promote your physical aesthetics, confidence, competitiveness, progressive spirit, and leadership ability altogether. Leadership ability on its own is just that but when combined with the rest of the above mentioned it is the characteristics of the alpha male. If you are motivated by what you see in other's that appear to be alpha males and you want to achieve those benefits for yourself, this is the only way of truly doing so.

Chapter 4: Benefits of Being the Alpha Male

The benefits of being the alpha male are robust. They come in every part of your daily life. These results can be classified in 3 distinct areas: individually, socially and professionally.

Individually

In your individual life you will feel better in your health, both physically and mentally. Your body will be in better shape because you'll be building your body in a healthy way. You'll be building functional muscle and not muscle on top of muscle on top of muscle, etc. This will bring vigor to your physique and to your mental state.

Secondly, you'll have a better sense of fulfilment. This will have a lot of meaningful benefits to you because of the reduction of stress due to the elimination of stress causing situations. You'll no longer be grasping at what you don't have or looking at what others have. You won't be relying on others. You'll be taking charge for yourself and you'll be relaxed in this state of self-sufficient.

Stress reduction is self-explanatory. Everyone would want this! Additionally, better health is also an easy to realize benefit. Less fatigue, more energy, less doctor visits and aesthetics are all benefits that come with working out more. These, in addition to social and professional success all lead to self-fulfillment which is easily the absolute goal of life in general terms.

Professionally

As mentioned in social benefits, these can further bolster your professional benefits. These social groups that take place in a work environment have potential. If they are willing to support you then that is opportunity for advancement.

Additionally, the most sought after skill or rather character trait of a good, productive manager is leadership. This is pinnacle to a good work environment. As an alpha male, you will seem inherently possess this attribute and fully embody the concept. This makes you the absolute optimal choice for that management position.

It doesn't just stop there. The reason that people want people with leadership skills is because that benefits the company! People with leadership skills motivate subordinates and get them to cooperate better together. They second guess your decisions less often because they respect you and are willing to take your suggestions to achieve better results.

Pair that with the competitive, progressive and knowledge base of the alpha male and your professional gains build exponentially. Working your way up the corporate ladder has never been so easy. If you are a salesman, people find it easier to buy from someone with confidence in their product. The biggest problem entrepreneurs have is doubt – the problem with new ideas isn't quality rather commitment – but you will not have that anymore. Increasing your topic education will also be a point you strive for.

Summary of Benefits

These benefits apply to all positions in the workplace. These benefits feed to all areas of life – individual, social and professional. Alpha males appear to be living happier lives for one really good reason. Because they are! All areas are promoted by this inner confidence and leadership trait.

Less stress, better health, less doubt, more friends, less opposition, and more professional reach. These are the benefits that you can get from becoming an alpha male yourself and this is what I want for you. I want to support you in this endeavor.

Conclusion

Something that you must remember is that once you make yourself an alpha male, you have to be wary of other alphas. Remember, each pack only has one alpha. A group cannot have too many because it will result with fighting and arguing. Everyone can't lead hand and hand because that is not the masculine alpha male thing to do. You want yourself surrounded by Beta males, your followers. That is where your ability will flourish.

For those of you that are motivated to become the alpha male, either from perceiving others or from reading this book, it is best to fully immerse yourself in it. You must completely achieve all of the abovementioned characteristics or else your image as the alpha male will be incomplete.

Apply these all together to really realize your ability to be the alpha male. Additionally, your transformation must be authentic because you cannot fake being the alpha male. You will be better off not doing this rather than giving an impartial attempt at it or doing so on faulty circumstances. You will save yourself time. However, for those that are absolutely committed to becoming the alpha male, motivated by the rewards of this persona and seek a change in their life, I wish you all the best. You will get the opportunity to take this task on yourself and then only you will get to reap the rewards.

A PREVIEW OF :

Cleaning And Organizing Hacks Vol.2

The Beginner's Guide To De-Cluttering Your Lifestyle in 14 Days Or Less

Disclaimer

- Although the author and publisher have made every effort to ensure that the information in this book was correct at press time, the author and publisher do not assume and hereby disclaim any liability to any party for any loss, damage, or disruption caused by errors or omissions, whether such errors or omissions result from negligence, accident, or any other cause.
- This book is not intended as a substitute for the medical advice of physicians. The reader should regularly consult a physician in matters relating to his/her health and particularly with respect to any symptoms that may require diagnosis or medical attention.

Copyright 2014 by karen Ashville - All rights reserved.

This document is geared towards providing exact and reliable information in regards to the topic and issue covered. The publication is sold with the idea that the publisher is not required to render accounting, officially permitted, or otherwise, qualified services. If advice is necessary, legal or professional, a practiced individual in the profession should be ordered.

- From a Declaration of Principles which was accepted and approved equally by a Committee of the American Bar Association and a Committee of Publishers and Associations.

In no way is it legal to reproduce, duplicate, or transmit any part of this document in either electronic means or in printed format. Recording of this publication is strictly prohibited and any storage of this document is not allowed unless with written permission from the publisher. All rights reserved.

The information provided herein is stated to be truthful and consistent, in that any liability, in terms of inattention or otherwise, by any usage or abuse of any policies, processes, or directions contained within is the solitary and utter responsibility of the recipient reader. Under no circumstances will any legal responsibility or blame be held against the publisher for any reparation, damages, or monetary loss due to the information herein, either directly or indirectly.

Respective authors own all copyrights not held by the publisher.

The information herein is offered for informational purposes solely, and is universal as so. The presentation of the information is without contract or any type of guarantee assurance.

The trademarks that are used are without any consent, and the publication of the trademark is without permission or backing by the trademark owner. All trademarks and brands within this book are for clarifying purposes only and are the owned by the owners themselves, not affiliated with this document.

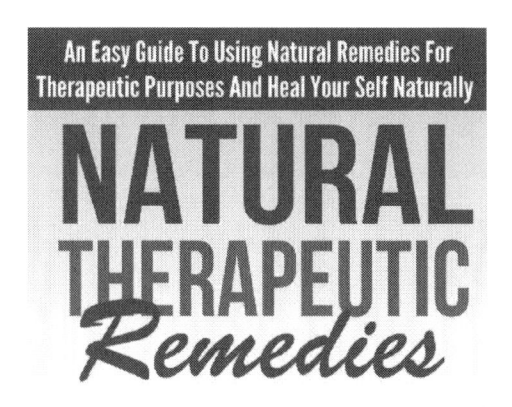

Your FREE Gift
Click Here

As a way of saying thank you,

Get your free natural therapeutic remedies report by clicking below.

What you'll receive

Enjoy the rest of the book!

Click here to get your Natural Therapeutic Remedies Report

Table Of Contents

Introduction

Chapter 1

Chapter 2

Chapter 3

Chapter 4

Chapter 5

Conclusion

Introduction

Has clutter taken control of your life? This is not surprising as each day seems to bombard us with new messages, files, tools, applications, toys, papers, deadlines, stress, and so much more. It can be quite overwhelming. Combined with our increasingly hectic schedules, it seems impossible to find the time to sort through it all. So the tendency is to allow things to pile up. It has become our regular way of life. Yet this is anything but wise since the bigger your clutter gets, the harder it is for you. Bills keep piling up. One day, you lose track of one and have to pay a late fee. You keep adding programs to your PC. It crashes and you now have to buy a new one. You find yourself stressed with all the tasks you have to do each day causing your very health to suffer.

Your life doesn't have to be a constant struggle to survive the chaos. You can change all this. What you will need to do is really dedicate yourself to bringing order to all aspects of your life. This includes de-cluttering your home, optimizing your computer, balancing your schedule, and relaxing your mind. While there is no magic spell to instantly fix everything, there are certain tips, steps, and routines guaranteed to help you deal with clutter. It will take time and effort, but it will all be worth it. So stop waiting for tomorrow. Take the first step to a clutter free life.

Chapter 1 An Uncluttered Home

Your home is not a storage area. Finding a pen should not feel like you're searching for buried treasure. Your home should be stress-free as much as possible, and it could be this way if you can get rid of clutter. You've probably been planning to do some cleaning for quite some time, but you just haven't gotten around to doing it yet, or perhaps you got discouraged every time you see just how high the piles of clutter are. Yes, organizing it all seems daunting, but by following a simple routine you will find that it is actually quite manageable.

The first thing you have to do is set aside some time to de-clutter. It can be either a whole Saturday morning or just ten minutes each night. The important thing is that once you've set your schedule, you stick to it like superglue.

Second, make sure that there are no distractions once you start cleaning. Turn off all of your unnecessary gadgets and keep them out of sight. This goes for your cellphone as well; place it in the next room. Text messages can wait until after you have finished cleaning, if it's important then the person will call. Also, don't stop to read an old magazine or article while you are working. The de-cluttering schedule should be strictly for decluttering.

Now that you've purged all distractions, you are ready to begin. Decide which room you want to clear first. One suggestion is the bedroom. This is your sanctuary, your most private place. It is the first thing you see when you wake up. Wouldn't it be nice to sleep without worrying about that large pile of clutter beside your bed toppling over and burying you alive? Look around your room. There may be clutter on the floor, tables, chairs, and even half the bed. Just keep calm and pick one pile of clutter at a time. It is best to start with smallest pile first to get into an easy rhythm. Once you start on a specific clutter pile stay on it. Focus on it until it is gone.

After clearing the first pile of clutter, dust the newly visible flat area. Isn't it nice to see it again? Take a close look and admire it; an actual flat space that you can now use again. Now imagine the rest of the room looking like that and you will be excited to move on to the next pile. Follow the same steps and start from the top. Don't touch the containers where you placed your stuff yet. Just continue to fill them out. Before you know it, all the clutter piles in the room will be gone. The room will look brand new, complete with chairs you can sit on, a table you can write on, a bed you can roll in, and a floor where you can walk on without having to watch your every step.

Once the things that once cluttered your room are in the four containers, you have to deal with them as soon as you can. First, pick up the "trash" container and throw it, and all of its contents, into the dumpster. All of these things have been weighing you down long enough. Throw them all out of your life forever.

After that, start sorting through the items in the "keep" box. Decide where you want to place each item. To make things easier, you need to group similar things together. For example, you can place all pens in the first drawer of your desk, and place papers on the second drawer. Put all the magazines on one side and all the books on another. You are creating the kind of room that you have always wanted, so you can choose where to put these things.